WELCOME TO SCREAM STREET®

WHERE MONSTROUSLY GREAT ADVENTURE LURKS AROUND EVERY CORNER...

When Luke Watson starts turning into a werewolf, Luke and his parents are relocated to Scream Street, a town inhabited by monsters. Luckily for Luke, he makes some fiendishly funny friends, and it's not long before they're caught up in a series of howlingly good adventures. One thing's for sure, Scream Street is the most spooktacular neighbourhood in the supernat

First published 2021 by Walker Entertainment
An imprint of Walker Books Ltd
87 Vauxhall Walk, London SE11 5HJ

2 4 6 8 10 9 7 5 3 1

Copyright © 2021 Coolabi Productions Limited
Based on the Scream Street series of books by Tommy Donbavand
Created in consultation with Coolabi Productions Limited
Text by Well-Crafted Content
Additional illustrations by Dynamo Limited

This book has been typeset in LD Horror Movie and Komika

Printed and bound by CPI Group (UK) Ltd

British Library Cataloguing in Publication Data: a catalogue record
for this book is available from the British Library

ISBN 978-1-5295-0380-7

www.walker.co.uk

SCREAM STREET®

THE SPOOKTACULAR JOKE BOOK

WHY DID THE ZOMBIE CHICKEN CROSS THE ROAD?

To get to The Other Side!

WALKER
ENTERTAINMENT

SCREAM STREET

1 THE GHOST TRAIN

2 HAUNTED HOUSE

3 EEFA'S EMPORIUM

4 SNEER HALL

FANGS FOR COMING!

LUKE WATSON

Smart and strong-willed
teenage werewolf.

CLEO FARR

Mummy, martial-arts
expert and adventurer.

RESUS NEGATIVE

Wannabe vampire with
a taste for sarcasm.

SUE & MIKE WATSON

Luke's petrified parents.

NILES FARR

Cleo's mummified dad.

ALSTON & BELLA NEGATIVE

Vampire parents of non-vampire, Resus.

SIX

Teenage monster with
a mix of talents.

DR F

Secretive scientist
with a sinister plan...

OTTO SNEER

Scream Street's
menacing mayor.

LUELLA

Trainee witch with a passion for potions.

EEFA EVERWELL

Luella's glamorous aunt, who's really a hideous witch.

DR SKULLY

Former laboratory skeleton turned teacher!

FARP

A goblin with truly terrible wind.

DOUG

Ultra-chilled zombie who's falling to pieces!

DIG

Half dog. Half skeleton. Loves to dig.

CONTENTS

$2+2=4$

$E=mc^2$

dszo

3.141

$H_2 + O = ?$

GHOUL SCHOOL

RGB v CMYK

WHAT'S THE FIRST THING DR SKULLY DOES WHEN HIS PUPILS ARRIVE?

He takes the register of deaths.

HOW DOES THE HUNCHBACK OF NOTRE DAME KNOW WHEN IT'S TIME FOR CLASS?

The bells ... the bells!

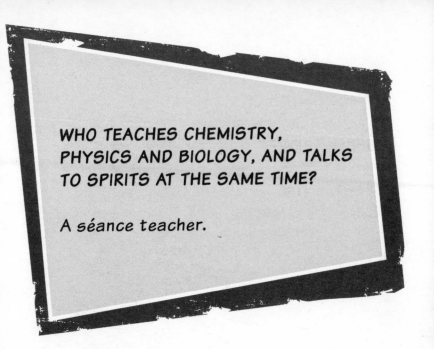

WHO TEACHES CHEMISTRY, PHYSICS AND BIOLOGY, AND TALKS TO SPIRITS AT THE SAME TIME?

A séance teacher.

DR SKULLY:

Where is your homework?

GHOST:

Sorry, Sir. My dog ate it.

DR SKULLY:

Don't make up excuses. I can see right through you.

WHY DO SPIRITS
HATE PE?

They don't want
to be exorcised.

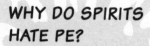

WHAT HAPPENS TO
WITCHES WHO ARE
TROUBLE IN CLASS?

They get ex-spelled.

WHY DID THE SKELETON SKIP MUSIC CLASS?

She forgot her trom-bone.

CLEO:

Wow! Where did you learn to make such amazing clothes and jewellery?

LUELLA:

In witchcraft, design and technology class.

WHY DO SKELETONS NEVER DO THEIR HOMEWORK?

They're bone idle.

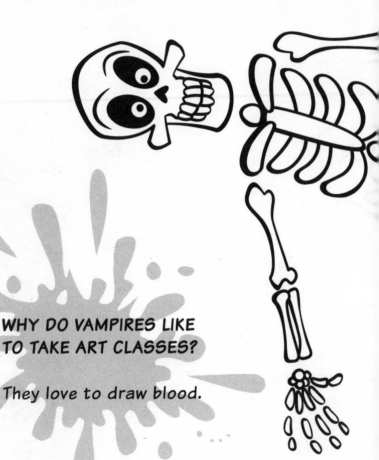

WHY DO VAMPIRES LIKE TO TAKE ART CLASSES?

They love to draw blood.

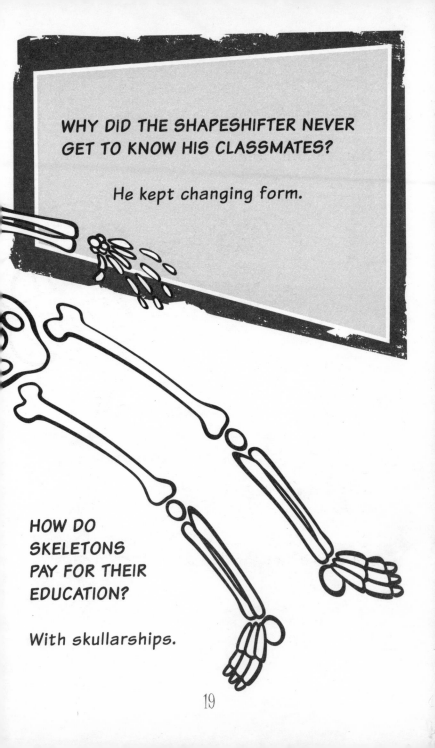

WHY DID THE SHAPESHIFTER NEVER GET TO KNOW HIS CLASSMATES?

He kept changing form.

HOW DO SKELETONS PAY FOR THEIR EDUCATION?

With skullarships.

DID YOU HEAR ABOUT THE WITCH WHO FLUNKED ALL HER EXAMS?

She couldn't spell.

DR SKULLY:

Don't roll your eyes at me when I give you homework, Doug.

DOUG:

Sorry, Sir. Could you roll them back, please?

WHAT DO MUMMIES CALL HISTORY CLASS?

Current affairs.

HOW DO GHOULISH TEACHERS EXPLAIN EXPERIMENTS TO PUPILS?

They demon-strate.

**WHAT DO BANSHEES
PLAY AT BREAK?**

Hide and shriek.

**WHAT DO WITCHES
EXCEL AT IN
MATHS CLASS?**

Algebra-cadabra!

**WHY WAS THE WITCH
GIVEN DETENTION?**

She kept cursing.

SCREAM STREET SCHOOL FOR YOUNG MONSTERS

– SCHOOL RULES –

1. Be punctual . . . by order of the late headmaster.

2. No running in the corridors . . . even if zombies are chasing you.

3. Uniforms must include blazer and tie and be wiped clean of blood.

4. No eating your classmates during lessons.

5. Be respectful to teachers, or they might put a curse on you.

6. Always bring your mummies to parents' evening.

7. Make sure you maintain a deathly silence in the library.

8. Rule breakers will answer to the Governing Bodies.

WHAT'S THE SCARIEST THING IN THE SCHOOL CANTEEN?

The food.

DID YOU HEAR ABOUT THE POLTERGEIST WHO SPOOKED A DINNER LADY?

He ended up with beans on ghost for lunch.

WHAT DO VAMPIRES STUDY INSTEAD OF HISTORY AND GEOGRAPHY?

Inhumanities.

WHY DID THE VAMPIRE GET EXPELLED?

He kept eating the dinner ladies for lunch.

**WHY DID RESUS
FAIL MATHS?**

He was relying on his
natural cape-ability
for the subject.

**WHY DID THE WITCH
KEEP FLYING AROUND
THE CLASSROOM?**

She wanted a higher
education.

WHY DOES DR SKULLY NEVER EAT IN THE SCHOOL CANTEEN?

He doesn't have the stomach for school dinners.

WHAT TYPE OF HANDWRITING DO WITCHES USE?

Cursive.

WHAT SHOULD YOU DO IF YOU FIND A MONSTER SITTING AT YOUR DESK?

Sit somewhere else.

LUKE:

How come you've been in the library all day?

DOUG:

It's this fella. He's a real bookworm!

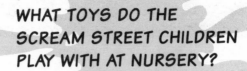

**WHAT TOYS DO THE
SCREAM STREET CHILDREN
PLAY WITH AT NURSERY?**

Transylvanian families.

WHAT'S A VAMPIRE'S FAVOURITE FRUIT?

Blood oranges.

It's neck-tarines, actually.

WHAT KIND OF RESTAURANT DO WEREWOLVES AVOID AT ALL COSTS?

Silver service.

WHAT'S A GHOST'S FAVOURITE CAKE?

A polter-g-iced finger.

WHAT DO SKELETONS ALWAYS HAVE FOR DINNER?

Spare ribs.

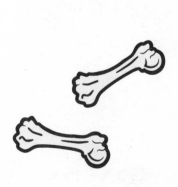

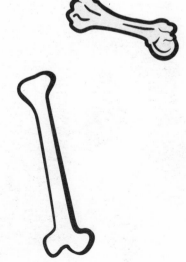

MR WATSON:

Eer, excuse me, waiter.
There's a spider in my soup.

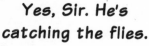

WAITER:

Yes, Sir. He's
catching the flies.

WHAT HAS A WAND,
AN EVIL CACKLE, A
CAULDRON AND LIVES
IN THE DESERT?

A sand-witch.

WHAT IS AN AMERICAN VAMPIRE'S FAVOURITE NATIONAL HOLIDAY?

Fangs-giving.

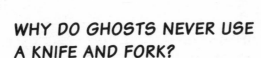

WHY DO GHOSTS NEVER USE A KNIFE AND FORK?

They prefer spooOOOooons!

There was a young vampire
called Wayne,

Who had trouble locating
a vein.

When he spotted a victim

His fangs only nicked him,

And he had to go
hungry again.

**HOW DO CANNIBALS
GREET PEOPLE?**

Pleased to eat you.

**WHAT DO GHOSTS
LIKE FOR PUDDING?**

I scream.

WHY DON'T MONSTERS EAT SWEETS?

They prefer unsavoury snacks.

LUKE:

Eer, waiter.
There's a hair
in my soup!

WAITER:

Well, keep your
paws away from
the bowl, Sir.

HOW DO WITCHES FLAVOUR THEIR STEWS?

With a little bit of sauce-ry.

WHICH TYPE OF CUISINE DO WITCHES LIKE?

Hex-Mex.

WHAT'S AN EVIL WITCH'S FAVOURITE RECIPE BOOK?

How to cook with children.

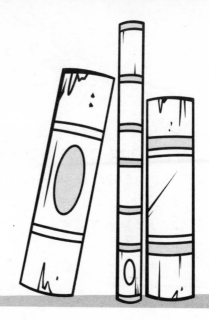

WHAT DO MUMMIES EAT CHIPS IN?

Embalm cakes.

WHAT DO MONSTERS LIKE EATING WITH THEIR FINGERS?

Toes.

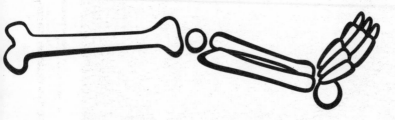

WHAT IS A GHOST'S FAVOURITE FAIRGROUND RIDE?

A roller-ghoster.

WHAT'S A MONSTER'S FAVOURITE SNACK?

Monster Munch.

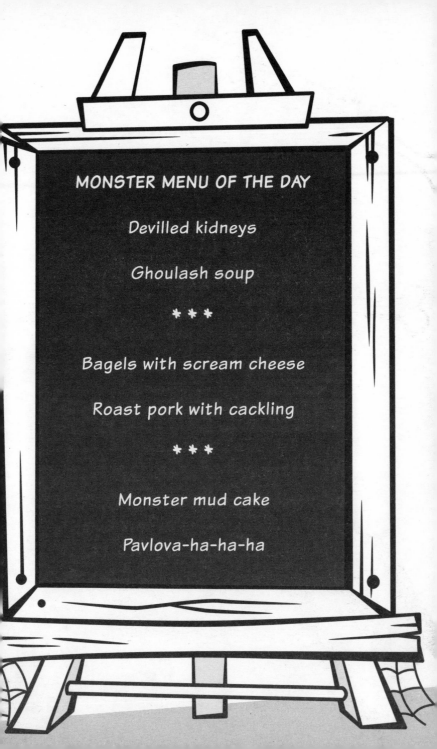

WHAT'S A MONSTER'S FAVOURITE DESSERT?

Key Slime Pie.

WHAT KIND OF BEANS DO WEREWOLVES PREFER?

Human beans.

WHAT DOES A VAMPIRE NEVER ORDER IN A RESTAURANT?

A steak.

LUKE:

We went to a zombie restaurant last night.

CLEO:

What was it like?

LUKE:

The food was okay, but the waiters were rotten.

WHAT DO GHOSTS SERVE UP FOR DESSERT?

TiramasooOOOooo.

WHAT DO GHOSTS EAT FOR DINNER?

Spook-hetti.

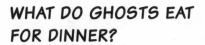

Ugh, that's pasta joke.

WHY IS FARP A TERRIBLE DINNER GUEST?

He does too much goblin.

BAT'S ENTERTAINMENT

LUKE:

I've been tuning in to a great radio
station where you can listen to
all your dead ancestors.

MRS WATSON:

Really? Where did you find that?

LUKE:

On medium wave.

WHICH TYPE OF MUSIC DO MUMMIES LIKE BEST?

Wrap music.

WHAT PLAY DO GHOSTS LOVE?

Romeo and Ghouliet.

HOW DO YOU CHEER UP A SAD POLTERGEIST?

Take them on a good fright out.

HOW DOES NO NAME STAY IN TOUCH WITH HIS MATES?

On Facelessbook.

WHY DO ZOMBIES WRITE THE UNDERWORLD'S BEST MUSIC?

They're great decomposers.

WHICH MUSIC FESTIVAL HAS EVERY VAMPIRE BEEN TO?

Bloodstock.

GROTIFY'S TOP 10
MOST SCREAMED SINGLES

1. Mummy in the Grave,
   by Drake-ula

2. Ips-witch Girl,
   by Dead Sheeran

3. Grooming the Werewolf,
   by Hairy Styles

4. Shallow (Grave),
   by Lady Gagaaaaaarrrrgggghhh

5. It's Not Usual,
   by Sir Tomb Bones

6. Time to Die,
   by Billie Ghoulish

7. Disturbia,
   by Rihanna-ha-ha-ha

8. Blinding Frights,
   by The Freakend

9. Zombie,
   by Miley Sirens

10. I Put a Spell on You,
    by Ann-eeee Lennox

WHY DON'T MUMMIES GO ON HOLIDAY?

They don't want to unwind.

WHAT DO MUMMIES SAY AT THE END OF FILMS?

"That's a wrap!"

WHERE DO MONSTERS WATCH VIDEOS?

GooTube.

WHAT DO GHOSTS DO FOR ENTERTAINMENT?

They go to the moooOOOoooOOOvies.

RESUS:

Why weren't you at the Brain Drain gig last night?

DOUG:

I had no body to go with.

DID YOU HEAR WHAT HAPPENED
WHEN THE COMPANY OF GHOSTS
PUT ON A PLAY?

Everyone got stage fright.

WHICH NEWSPAPER DO
VAMPIRES NEVER LOOK AT?

The Mirror.

DID YOU HEAR ABOUT THE
ZOMBIE WHO FELL INTO A HOLE?

It was a grave situation.

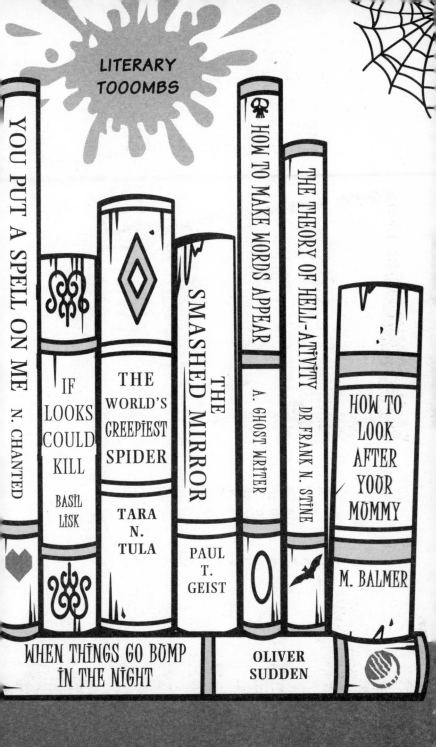

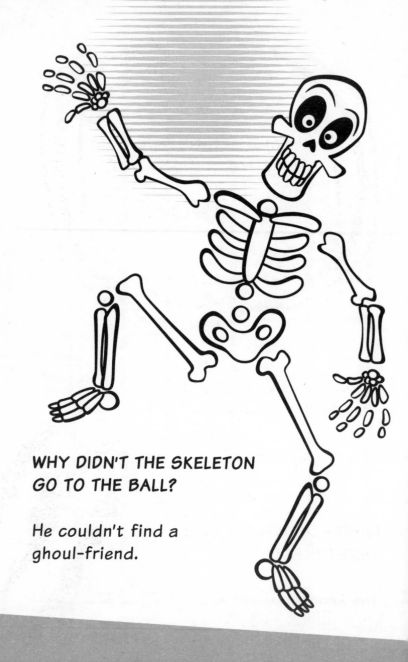

WHY DIDN'T THE SKELETON GO TO THE BALL?

He couldn't find a ghoul-friend.

WHAT DO MONSTERS WEAR FOR A NIGHT OUT?

Chainsaw mascara.

WHAT DO VAMPIRES LIKE TO EAT ON HOLIDAY?

The other tourists.

WHERE DO WEREWOLVES TAKE HOLIDAYS?

The kennels.

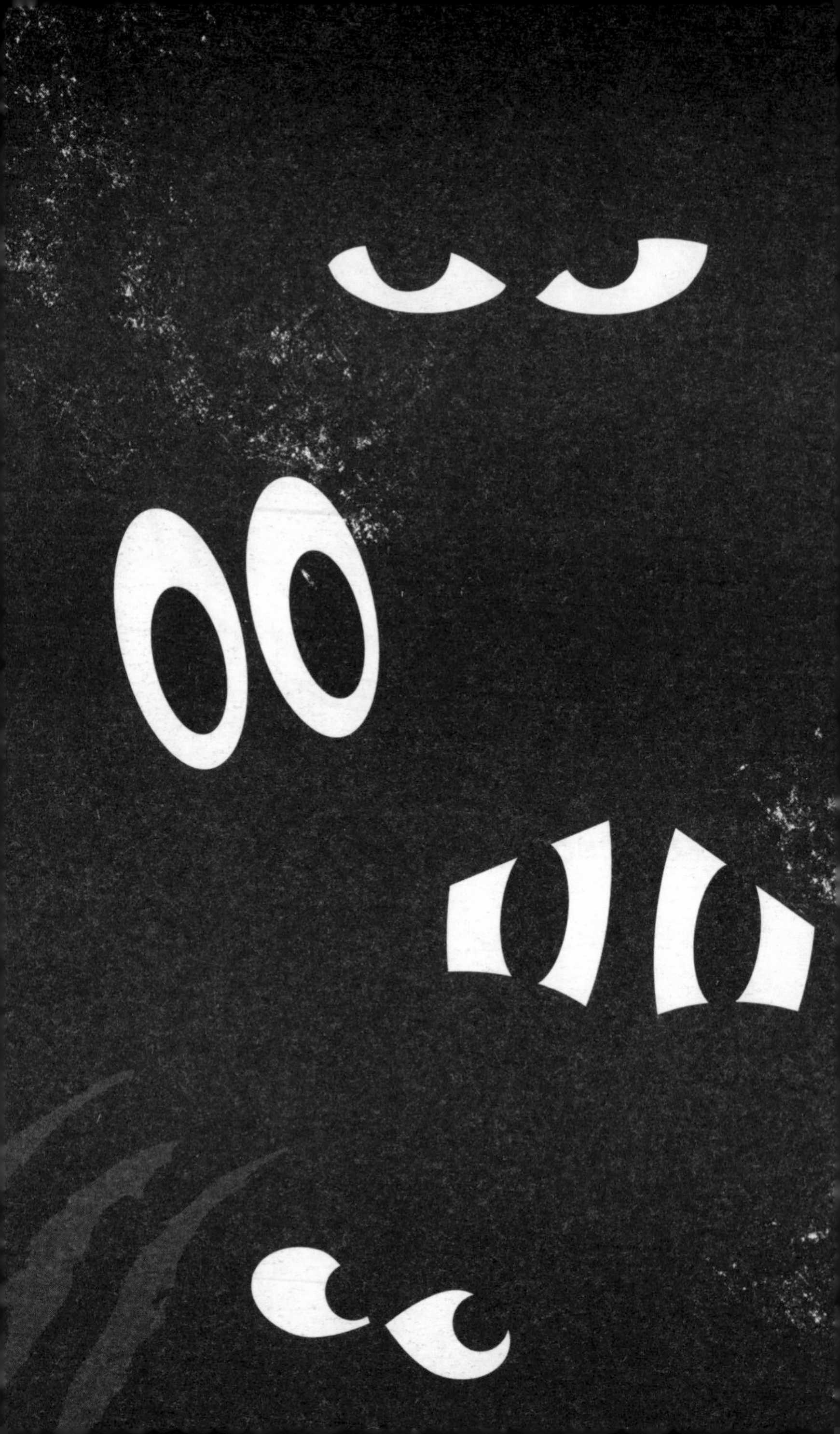

NIGHTMARISH
CREATURES

WHAT'S WHITE, FLOATS DOWN THE STAIRS AND GOES _BOOM!_?

An exploding ghost.

WHAT PART OF THE STREET DO ZOMBIES LIVE ON?

The dead end.

WHICH DOG IS THE BEST COMPANION FOR A WITCH?

A labra-cadabra-dor.

DID YOU HEAR ABOUT THE WEREWOLF WHO LOST HIS CLOTHES?

He was a barewolf.

WHAT DO YOU GET IF YOU CROSS A VAMPIRE WITH AN ICE MUMMY?

Frostbite.

WHAT DO YOU CALL A SCOTTISH ZOMBIE?

MacAbre.

WHAT'S THE ONLY PLACE BIG ENOUGH FOR A WHOLE FAMILY OF WEREWOLVES?

A werehouse.

WHAT DO YOU GET IF YOU CROSS A WITCH'S CAT AND A SPIDER?

An *octopuss.*

WHY DID THE CHICKEN CROSS THE ROAD?

It was being chased by Dig.

SO, WHY DIDN'T DIG CROSS THE ROAD?

He didn't have the guts.

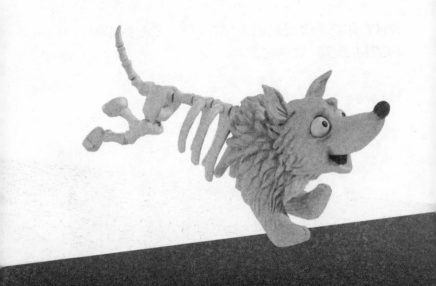

There was a young witch
named Pat,
Who was given a new
black cat.
It sat on her broom
And whizzed round the room,
And knocked off her
black pointy hat.

**WHY DID THE MONSTER GET BANNED
FROM SOCIAL MEDIA?**

He was a terrible troll.

DID YOU HEAR
WHAT HAPPENED
WHEN LUELLA
SPILLED A POTION
ON HER TEDDY?

It turned into a
grizzly bear.

HOW DID THE
WITCH LOOSE
HER TOAD?

She frogot them.

TOP TIPS FOR TAKING CARE
OF YOUR PET MONSTER

1. Buy a strong cage. If you can't find one big enough, try keeping your pet monster in the cellar, and barricade the door.

2. Ensure your monster has somewhere comfortable to sleep, like a coffin ... or bed of nails.

3. Choose the right habitat. Monsters like dark spaces, such as under your bed or in the wardrobe.

4. Let your monster gnaw bones to keep their teeth sharp, but don't feed them your annoying brother or sister, as your parents are bound to notice.

5. Clean your monster's cage regularly, just remember to make sure you don't get locked in with them.

6. And finally, remember: a monster is for life, not just for Halloween.

DID YOU HEAR ABOUT THE VAMPIRE FROG?

It had a long croak.

WHAT DO YOU GET IF YOU CROSS A MONSTER AND AN ANCIENT ROMAN?

An ogre in a toga.

**WHAT DIES, THEN STINGS
YOU AFTERWARDS?**

A zom-bee.

**WHAT KIND OF BEAST
ALWAYS WANTS
WHAT YOU HAVE?**

A green-eyed
monster.

A ghost who wasn't so bright,
Tried haunting a mansion
at night.
He got stuck in the loo
And then tried to say "boo",
But the echo gave him a fright!

**WHY DID THE ZOMBIE CHICKEN
CROSS THE ROAD?**

To get to The Other Side.

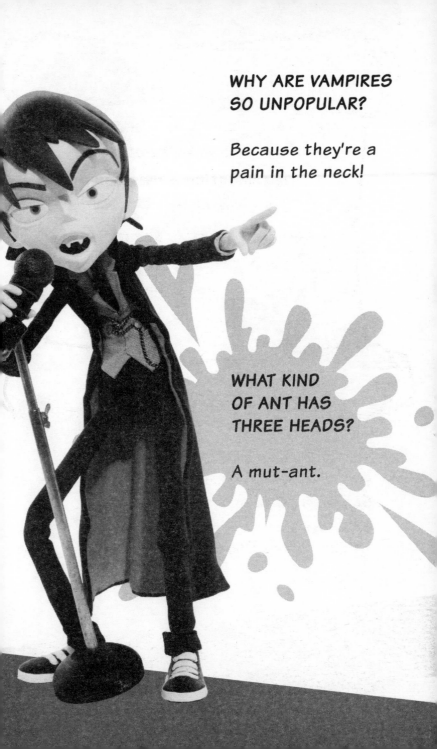

WHY ARE VAMPIRES SO UNPOPULAR?

Because they're a pain in the neck!

WHAT KIND OF ANT HAS THREE HEADS?

A mut-ant.

WHAT DO YOU CALL A MUMMIFIED SNAKE?

A wrap-tile.

WHY DID EEFA RECOGNIZE A BAT?

He was a little familiar.

KNOCK, KNOCK

Who's there?

NORA

Nora who?

NORA YERBONES!

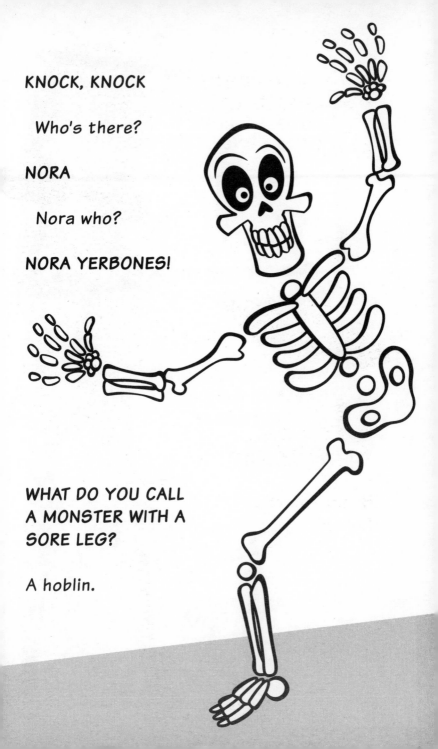

WHAT DO YOU CALL
A MONSTER WITH A
SORE LEG?

A hoblin.

WHAT SHOES DO GHOSTS
LIKE TO WEAR?

BoooOOOoooOOOoots.

WHAT KIND OF MONSTER IS
GREEN, STICKY AND CRAWLS
UP YOUR NOSE?

A bogeyman.

HOW DO YOU KNOW WHEN DOUG'S UPSET?

He puts his head in his hands.

HOW DOES A HEADLESS HORSEMAN SAY GOODBYE?

"I'll beheading off then!"

SPOOKTATOR SPORTS

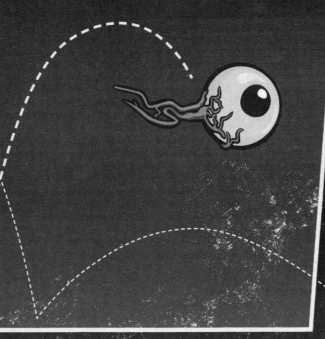

WHAT'S A GHOST'S FAVOURITE TYPE OF CRICKET?

Day-fright matches.

WHY DO SHAPE-SHIFTERS LIKE CRICKET?

They love going into bat.

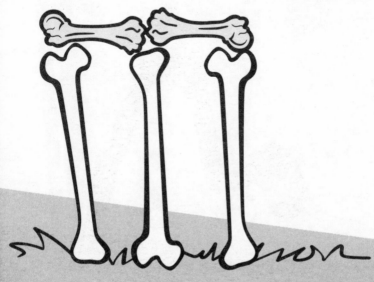

WHY WAS THERE NO WINNER IN THE ZOMBIE RACE?

It was a dead heat.

HOW DO MONSTERS KEEP FIT?

They jog on a dread-mill.

WHAT'S A SPIDER'S FAVOURITE PASTIME?

Fly fishing.

WHY DON'T VAMPIRES LIKE HORSE RACING?

They're terrified of sweep-stakes.

WHAT SPORT DO HAIRY MONSTERS LIKE PLAYING?

Bigfoot-ball.

WHAT'S THE ONLY SPORT GIANTS CAN PLAY?

Squash.

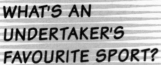

WHAT'S AN UNDERTAKER'S FAVOURITE SPORT?

Casket-ball.

WHICH SPORT DO SKELETONS EXCEL AT?

Sculling.

WHAT DO ZOMBIES WEAR UNDER THEIR TRACKSUIT BOTTOMS?

Undead-pants.

SCREAM STREET SPOOKTACULAR SPORTS COMPETITION

Walk, skulk or fly down to the sporting event of the year and watch spooktator sports like:

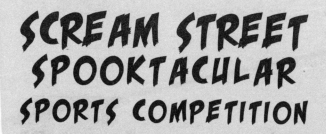

HANDBALL: marvel as Doug throws his hand (literally) over the net.

JUDO: can reigning champion, Cleo, once again tie her opponents in knots?

SPRINT RACE: will Farp win the goblin gas-powered sprint race? And, can the crowd hold their breath until the race is over?

WHAT DO YOU GET IF YOU PUT A LOAD OF BANSHEES IN BOATS?

A wailing regatta.

WHAT'S THE BIGGEST SPORTING EVENT OF THE YEAR FOR GHOSTS?

The Supernatural Bowl.

WHAT SPORT DO ZOMBIES LIKE TO PLAY?

Eyes hockey.

WHAT HAPPENS WHEN VAMPIRE FOOTBALL MATCHES GO TO PENALTIES?

It ends in sudden death.

WHAT'S DR F'S FAVOURITE TYPE OF FOOTBALL?

Six-a-side.

WHAT DO YOU CALL A VAMPIRE WHO'S RUBBISH AT GOLF?

Count Hackula.

WHY WAS THE SUPERSTAR WEREWOLF ALLOWED TO LEAVE HIS MONSTERBALL TEAM?

Because of the claws in his contract.

WHICH POSITION DO GHOSTS LIKE PLAYING IN NETBALL?

Ghoul attack.

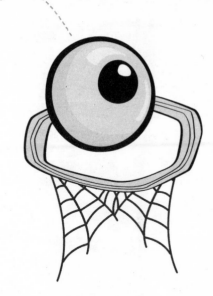

WHY DO SPORTS STARS HATE GHOSTS?

They're always booing them off.

WHY DID THE WITCH TAKE HER BROOMSTICK TO THE FOOTBALL FIELD?

She was playing sweeper.

WHY DO WITCHES LIKE BEING PART OF FOOTBALL CROWDS?

They love the en-chanting.

RESUS:

Why are Luella, Six and Doug doing that scary dance on the touchline?

CLEO:

They're fearleaders.

WHAT MAKES GHOSTS GOOD AT SPORTS?

Team spirit.

WHAT DO WITCHES RACE INSTEAD OF CARS?

Vroomsticks.

WHAT SPORT DO WEREWOLVES LOVE?

Ten-pin howling.

WHAT RUINS A ROUND OF GOLF?

A bogeyman at every hole.

FEELING
ROTTEN

LUKE:

What have you got against maggots anyway?

DOUG:

They just really get under my skin, dude.

LUELLA:

Doctor, doctor. A warlock put an itching spell on me.

DR F:

I can't cure that, but Witch Hazel might help.

WHAT HAPPENS TO GHOULS WHEN THEY GET A FEVER?

They have creep-less nights.

There was a young skeleton,
Pete,
Who fell on his face in
the street.
The hard paving stones
Scattered all of his bones,
And a dog ran away
with his feet.

RESUS:

I was sick last night so
I went to the doctor.

LUKE:

Which doctor?

RESUS:

No, just a regular one.

HOW DO YOU KNOW WHEN
A GHOST IS UNWELL?

They go achoooOOOooo!

WHY DO WITCH DOCTORS ALWAYS PRESCRIBE HERBAL REMEDIES?

Because they're super-natural.

DID YOU HEAR ABOUT THE WITCH WHO KEPT FLYING ROUND IN CIRCLES ON HER BROOMSTICK?

She had dizzy spells.

WHY ARE THERE SECURITY GUARDS ON THE GRAVEYARD GATES?

Because people are just dying to get in.

LUELLA:

Doctor, doctor. I gave my cauldron a stir and now I can't stop throwing up.

DOCTOR:

Sounds like a bad case of potion sickness.

WHY COULDN'T THE ZOMBIE WALK?

He had a dead leg.

WHAT DO ZOMBIE DOGS SUFFER FROM?

Worms.

CLEO:

Ugh, I'm just burning up with this fever.

DOCTOR:

Oh dear. That sounds like hell.

GHOST:

Doctor, doctor, I've... oooOOOoooOOOoooohhhh!

DOCTOR:

Sounds like a bout of moaning sickness to me.

FRIGHTFUL FIRST AID TIPS

- If the patient has no pulse, do not be alarmed ... they may not have a heart.

- When giving mouth-to-mouth resuscitation, beware of fangs.

- If treating vampires, never call in the Red Cross.

- Mummy First Aid kits should contain: bandages, finger bandages, eye bandages, triangular bandages, conforming bandages, crepe bandages and safety pins.

- Place unconscious patients in the recovery position, except vampires who should go on their back with arms crossed over their chest.

RESUS:

Doctor, doctor. I think I'm going mad!

DOCTOR:

Don't worry. You're just a bit batty.

WHAT'S THE BEST WAY TO KNOW IF YOU'LL BE SCARED IN THE FUTURE?

Read a horror-scope.

CLEO:

Doctor, doctor. I think there's something wrong with my bandages.

DOCTOR:

It's probably nothing. Try not to get too wrapped up in your worries.

WHAT DO YOU SAY WHEN A WITCH SNEEZES?

Curse you!

DR SKULLY:

I had to use a tranquiliser
dart to sedate Luke.

RESUS:

So, now he's an unaware wolf?

DOCTOR:

I'm afraid that we can't find
anything wrong with you.

OTTO:

Can I get a second opinion?

DOCTOR:

Of course. I'm afraid
you're rather ugly.

WHY WAS THE DOCTOR CALLED TO SNEER HALL?

People kept saying it had a haunted look about it.

WHAT DID THE WEREWOLF SAY WHEN HE STUBBED HIS PAW?

Ow-ooooooooooohhhhh!

FARP:

> Doctor, Doctor.
> Can you give me
> something for wind?

DOCTOR:

> You could try
> this kite...

WHAT DO SICK GHOSTS SUFFER FROM?

Wailments.

**WHAT DO YOU GET IF YOU CROSS
A VAMPIRE WITH A TEACHER?**

A blood test.

BELLA NEGATIVE:

Doctor, doctor.
My coughing
stops me sleeping.

DOCTOR:

Well, maybe try sleeping
in a bed instead.

WHY DON'T VAMPIRES VISIT BLOOD BANKS?

They'd miss the thrill of the chase.

WHAT HAPPENS TO GHOSTS AFTER THEY UNDERGO SURGERY?

They get phantom pains.

SIX:

Doctor, doctor. I've been
feeling really flat.

DR F:

Sounds like you just need
a holiday to recharge
your batteries.

COMMUNITY

SPIRITS

WHAT DO WITCHES DO WHEN THEY GET LONELY?

Look for broom-mates.

DID YOU HEAR ABOUT THE GHOST WHO RAN A MARKET STALL?

He was a scaremonger.

WHO LAUGHS IN THE FACE OF DEATH?

The Grin Reaper.

WHAT KIND OF MAYOR IS SIR OTTO SNEER?

Your worst night-mayor.

KNOCK, KNOCK

Who's there?

ISLA.

Isla who?

ISLA BITE
YOUR NECK.

WHERE DO VAMPIRES
KEEP THEIR MONEY?

The blood bank.

KNOCK, KNOCK

Who's there?

DOM.

Dom who?

DOM-DOM-DOOOOM!

HOW DO YOU STOP WORRYING ABOUT
MONSTERS UNDER YOUR BED?

Sleep on the floor.

DID YOU HEAR ABOUT THE
VAMPIRE WHO APPEARED
IN COURT?

He gave the tooth, the
whole tooth, and nothing
but the tooth.

HOW DO GOBLINS GET AROUND TOWN?

In monster trucks.

LUKE:

Hi, Dr Skully! Want to hear a joke about a skeleton?

DR SKULLY:

No! Don't tell me. It's just too close to the bone.

WHAT DO YOU CALL A GHOST IN A HURRY?

A wraith against time.

WHY CAN YOU ALWAYS TRUST A MUMMY WITH A SECRET?

You know they'll keep it under wraps.

WHY WERE THE
GHOSTS KICKED OUT
OF THEIR HOUSE?

It was re-possessed.

KNOCK, KNOCK

Who's there?

ALBIE.

Albie who?

ALBIE BACK TO HAUNT YOU...

HOW TO BE A MONSTER HIT ON ANTISOCIAL MEDIA

1. Post petrifying pictures on
   MONSTERGRAM

2. Do dreadful dances on
   TIKSHOCK

3. Frighten a friend on
   FACEBooOOOOoo

4. Feature fiendish footage on
   EWWTUBE

5. Snap a spooky selfie on
   BATCHAT

WHAT DO YOU CALL IT WHEN 500 ZOMBIES EMERGE FROM A CEMETERY?

A grave situation.

WHAT DO VAMPIRES CALL IT WHEN BURGLARS RAID WHILE THEY'RE SLEEPING?

Daylight robbery.

WHY DID CLEO NEED TO FIND DR SKULLY?

She had a bone to pick with him.

RESUS:

How does Luke trim his hair after a full moon?

CLEO:

Eclipse it.

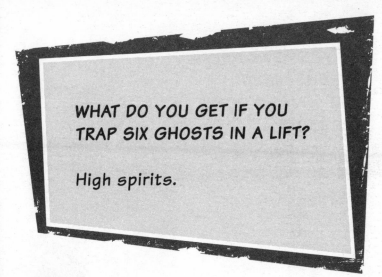

WHAT DO YOU GET IF YOU TRAP SIX GHOSTS IN A LIFT?

High spirits.

WHAT DO VAMPIRES AND MUMMIES SPEND IN SHOPS?

Crypt-ocurrency.

WHAT DO YOU CALL A MUMMY WHO'S BEEN KNIGHTED BY THE QUEEN?

Sir Cophagus.

DID YOU HEAR ABOUT
THE SHAPESHIFTER
THAT WALKED DOWN
A STREET?

They turned into
a lane.

WHAT'S THE
QUICKEST
WAY TO THE
UNDERWORLD?

The Hellevator.

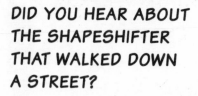

HOW DO GHOSTS TRAVEL FROM FLOOR TO FLOOR?

By scare-case.

VOICE:

KNOCK, KNOCK.

NILES:

Who's there?

VOICE:

THE GRIM REAPER

NILES:

Go next door. I died centuries ago.

WHY ARE VAMPIRES LIKE YOUR GRANNY'S TEETH?

They come out at night.

WHY CAN'T GHOSTS TRAVEL ON PLANES?

They've already departed.

KNOCK, KNOCK

Who's there?

DONNA

Donna who?

DONNA LOOK UNLESS YOU'RE REALLY BRAVE!

DISCOVER THE FRIGHTFULLY FUNNY FIRST SCREAM STREET ADVENTURE!

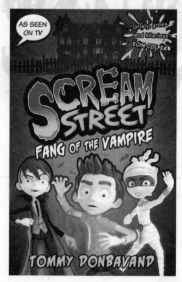

After Luke Watson transforms into a werewolf, he and his parents are moved by the Government Housing of Unusual Lifeforms (G.H.O.U.L.) to Scream Street. Luke soon makes friends with sarcastic vampire, Resus Negative and martial-arts mummy, Cleo Farr. When he learns that finding six powerful relics will open a doorway out of the street, he and his new friends set out to find the first one: the vampire's fang. But with Otto Sneer determined to thwart him at every turn, will Luke even get past the first hurdle alive?

Find out more at

WWW.SCREAMSTREET.CO.UK